BLACKWOOD YESTERDAY

in photographs
including the villages of
CWMFELINFACH, YNYSDDU, PONTLLANFRAITH, OAKDALE, CEFN FFOREST, FLEUR-DE-LYS, PENGAM, ABERBARGOED, ARGOED, MARKHAM AND HOLLYBUSH

Ewart Smith, M.Sc.

Foreword by
Peter G. Bullen, D.F.C.

Book 3

Old Bakehouse Publications

Abertillery

First published in May 1998
Reprinted in June 2003
Reprinted in October 2016

ISBN 1 874538 76 X

Published in the U.K. by
Old Bakehouse Publications
Church Street,
Abertillery, Gwent NP13 1EA
Telephone: 01495 212600 Fax: 01495 216222
Email: theoldbakeprint@btconnect.com

Made and printed in the UK
by Bakehouse Print Limited.

British Library Cataloguing in Publication Data: a catalogue
record for this book is available from the British Library.

Foreword

by Peter G Bullen, D.F.C.
former Chairman of Bedwellty U D C and Mayor of Islwyn

"Come let us walk down memory lane
It's a wonderful place to be;
For there it seems we dream our dreams
Of the days we used to know.
It stretches on for many a mile
The end we cannot see;
So come along with cheerful song
And walk awhile with me."

The first verse of *Memory Lane*, a poem by F J Harding, reminds us of the magic of memory and Ewart Smith's first two volumes entitled *Blackwood Yesterday* rekindled all sorts of memories for people of all ages.

Half a century ago I came from Cambridgeshire to earn a living in South Wales, and a year later my wife and I returned from our honeymoon to live in Gordon Road. Little did we realise then how our lives and the town of Blackwood would become so intertwined. As recently as 1995 I was privileged to be elected to the new Town Council, an organisation which seeks to preserve the identity of the town and its environs, and to further its interests within the new Caerphilly County Borough.

Even though I am a relatively 'new boy' I have witnessed the evolution of the town from the austerity following the Second World War, through the demise of the valley's traditional industries to today's bustling community with its enviable reputation for quality of life and modern industry.

Through *Blackwood Yesterday* those of us who are now the older generation have our failing memories revived and for the younger generation and those still to come, there is no doubt that the history that will shape their futures is preserved for posterity.

I have great pleasure in commending Ewart's third book in the series and trust that it will not be his last to record the people, events and places where so many have chosen to live their lives.

"So if at times the way is dark
And sad your thoughts may be
Come once again down memory lane
And walk awhile with me."

Contents

Introduction

The reception given to the first two books in the *Blackwood Yesterday* series clearly suggests that they satisfy a need. Book 2 was published just over two years ago and since then a significant amount of new material has become available which has prompted this book.

If you travelled up the Sirhowy valley in the years immediately after the Second World War the chances were that you were aboard either a Western Welsh or a Red & White bus. You slowed down at the Plaza corner (scene of much social activity) opposite Pontllanfraith bottom station, possibly waited for a few minutes for the gates of the railway level-crossing to open and proceeded to Blackwood along a route parallel to the railway. There was not a single roundabout in sight! As you entered the town, Libanus Chapel, with the only graveyard in the town, stood on the left and a little way beyond on the right was Salter & Roberts, Upholsterers. (Mr Salter kept dozens of the most exotic birds.) At the bottom of Gordon Road, you came to the Parrot Hotel. In the West End buildings opposite were The Beehive, Houghtons Cycle & Radio store, Southerleys and Ellaways, both hairdressers, Austin Morgan (grocer), Palmer (butcher) and Resteghini's, an Italian Cafe with its Juke Box and back room for favoured customers. As you drove through the town you became aware that the street was wide for a valley town (the railway used to run through it); that there seemed to be bus stands everywhere, and you were conscious of the large number of pubs - The Butchers Arms (now The Porters), The George, The Forresters (now the New Forresters), The Royal Oak (on Fads site), The Crown (where Tesco's is), The Tredegar Arms (now The Mill), The Red Lion and The Carpenters Arms (just beyond Gibbons) - and the number of grocers' shops - Peglers, Jones & Porter, Star Supply Stores, Home & Colonial, D J Evans, Chappells, Cromwell Jones, Evan Hopkins (Royal Stores), Miss Walters (near The Carpenters) and Mrs Davies (Rock Shop).

The local butchers were Woodwards, Browns, Dewhursts and Rossers; while Colemans, Jones and Arnolds were the greengrocers and fruiterers. Sumptions, Thomas and Jenkins were the chemists and we had three other Italian Cafes - Conti's Palace Cafe, Rossi's Square Cafe and Minoli's Everybody's Cafe. We also had Stokes's Dorothy Cafe: this became Lusardi's. There was Tudor Evans (ironmonger), Southcotts (decorating materials), Roberts (printer) and Templemans and The Bargoed Radio for both cycles and radio. The larger shops in the town were Jones & Richards (The Fashion Centre of the Valleys), Leslie Stores (now Poundstretcher), The London Hosiery (the block opposite Poundstretcher), Tidals Stores (our 1940s Woolworths!) and Babers. On The Square were The Bargoed Emporium and Glanfryd, Edmund Edmunds's imposing dressed stone detached house (Woolworths' site), and further north The Stute - the social Mecca for many young valley folk on Wednesday and Saturday evenings where the dances, compered by Harry Brooks, were such an attraction. A few hundred yards beyond The Stute was The Drill Hall, built as a base for The Volunteers in the middle of the 19th century and the home of the first State school in the town. Adjacent to the Drill Hall was Budd's New Rock Colliery, from which the coal trucks crossed the road to the main line. St Margaret's Church, was surrounded by the colliery, the West Mon bus depot and Brown's Foundry, which could be a spectacular sight on a dark cold winter's afternoon. Beyond this the road narrowed, the Carpenters Arms stood on one side and the railway station on the other.

The chapels were not as conspicuous as the pubs. The Methodist Church near The Square, Mount Pleasant English Baptist Church on Cefn Road and the Presbyterian Church in Bridge Street were all slightly removed from the main thoroughfare, as was the former Primitive Methodist Church (now The Little Theatre), which was still full of the emergency supplies stored there during the war. The Maxime and Capitol cinemas were invariably packed out, sporting queues several hundred yards long on most Fridays and Saturdays. Greater dignity was associated with the Maxime than the Capitol because of 'Sarge', a commissionaire who was always immaculately dressed in his blue and yellow uniform. At this time the Pathé News, our only way of seeing the news, was shuttled between the two cinemas several times a day.

How different things are today. The overall impression as one travels along the High Street concerns the number of Estate Agents, Building Societies, Travel Agents and Charity shops. The business of the High Street has changed significantly. This book is an attempt to capture and record a little of the way of life and atmosphere of yesteryear in this small corner of our county.

CHAPTER 1

Blackwood Town

1. A very early view (c 1904) of Blackwood High Street looking north. The three-storey building on the right is the George Hotel, next to which is a large open space where the market was held. The Royal Oak overlooks the market area.

2. The single track bridge crossing the Sirhowy river linking Blackwood with Woodfieldside. The Rock and Fountain Inn is on the right, Jerusalem Chapel (established c1839 by a breakaway group from Penmaen Independent Chapel) directly behind, and the Gas Works and Glan yr Afon Park to the left of the picture.

3. A general view of Blackwood from the west c1910 showing the Wesleyan Chapel which was destroyed by fire in 1915. There are no buildings to the east of Cefn Road, that is, no Pentwyn Road, South View Road or Pentwyn Avenue.

4. Blackwood High Street at the turn of the century. A cart stands outside Woodward's original shop while, on the other side of the dirt road, a large group of well turned out children congregate near the newly painted Royal Oak Hotel. The boys wear long trousers, caps and wide stiff white collars.

5. Another view of Blackwood High Street taken during the first decade of this century, this time looking south. On the left are the premises of A T Broadlick, Surgeon Dentist!! The gas for the street lighting is supplied by the Blackwood Gas Company owned by Richard Morris and manufactured in his gasworks behind his shop (Present day Tidals Stores).

6. Looking north along Blackwood High Street c1935. The road has by now been covered with tarmacadam, electric street lighting has been introduced and a few cars are beginning to appear. The side wall of the present Tidals Stores building advertises films at the Palace cinema - a building that now houses Babers' furniture store.

7. The Square, Blackwood c1915, showing the entrance to the newly constructed gentlemen's underground lavatory.

8. Blackwood High Street looking north in 1948. A serviceman pushes his bicycle past The Star Supply Stores and the Home & Colonial (both grocers). Films are advertised for the Maxime and Capitol cinemas. Note the bus-stands on both sides of the street - this was long before the building of the Bus Station.

9. A 1960s picture of the High Street. To the right is Tudor Evans (Ironmongers), R E & A G Thomas (Chemists) and The Bookshop (also belonging to the Thomas brothers). Further up the street a Jacobs biscuit van delivers to The Star Supply Stores, while to the left is the Maxime cinema, Suter and Bailey (Furnishers) and the Butchers Arms, which subsequently was renamed The Porters.

10. Blackwood High Street on a warm sunny afternoon in 1949. The Post Office, built in the 1920s, is still opposite the Maxime. On the extreme right is M L Jenkins the Chemist (later to become Meudells) and next to it Lamberts the Clothiers, established in 1933.

11. Blackwood High Street looking south from the bottom of Woodbine Road (formerly known as Morris Lane after Richard Morris's shop which was on the High Street at the entrance to the lane) in the late 1940s. To the left is The London Hosiery, formerly the drapery business of A P Hughes. The stone balustrade at the top of the building was subsequently removed, and the business closed to be replaced by several separate units. The Electricity Showroom on the right was removed when the new shopping centre was built. This was to improve access for the large supermarket lorries. On the nearby lamppost is a sign marked 'Ladies' directing those in need to the Ladies' Toilet a short distance up Morris Lane.

12. Looking from the railway line towards Woodfield. Several people are walking along Bridge Street. On the left, at the south end of William Street, is the chapel of the Presbyterian Church in Wales. This was built in 1910 at a cost of £400 and could seat 150. The Rock and Fountain Inn is in the centre of the picture.

13. The Forresters' Arms with its window boxes and shutters before John Williams (Tobacconist) was taken down to facilitate a pedestrian entrance to the new shopping centre.

14. It was possible to photograph this scene (taken in 1991) only between the time of the fire that destroyed Stevens Value and the construction of the Argos building. The central shop in the block was the Gas Showroom until a new showroom was opened in the shopping centre. This is the largest symmetrical building in the town. It was built c1904 and called Bank Buildings, probably because it was the location of the National and Provincial Bank. The only other bank in the town at that time was Lloyds.

15. This picture shows a quiet scene, but every Friday and Saturday the area was a hive of activity. It was here that for many years in the 1970s and '80s the Open Air Market was held until the ground was required for the new shopping centre. The building in the centre was a betting office.

16. The demolition of the Capitol cinema, the building originally being used for live performances. When these ceased to be well patronised it became an Indoor Market and later a cinema. Kwik Save supermarket was subsequently built on the site.

17. The Masonic Hall, Blackwood, built c1912 as The Workingmen's Home by John William Ebley on land he had leased from Viscount Tredegar in August 1911. It was known locally as Ebley's Lodging House, and is shown here in the winter of 1973. Islwyn Masonic Lodge at Blackwood was formed in 1925 and met in the Palace Buildings adjacent to the Palace cinema (now Babers) until it moved to its present site when the building became available at the end of World War II. The other lodging house was Bowen's, at the south end of the town. It is recorded that as late as 1957 Bill Bowen charged 1/9 (about 9p) a night for one of his ten beds. For that you got a pair of sheets, a pillow case and a blanket. The only light in the upstairs sleeping area came from the streetlamps and moon, the toilet was one of two buckets in the middle of the floor, and in the morning you sat around a table set on a flagstone floor with several squashed blackpats (beetles) under your feet.

18. The junction of Pentwyn Road, South View Road and Pentwyn Avenue in the early 1920s. There are no trees around the cenotaph. A mother and children have just negotiated the shallow steps on the corner which were removed when the corner was 'rounded' to make it easier for heavy vehicles to turn.

19. A familiar sight to older people of the area as they walked from the top of Gordon Road towards Lanes Corner. Many a local child collected tadpoles here in times past. While this was the scene in the years before and during World War II great changes have taken place since. The tree and pond have long since been removed, the large private estate of Bonnie View has been built on the fields to the left, and new housing is in the process of being built on the ground to the right.

20. Lovers' Lane, Blackwood, c1905. This is believed to be the lane that leads from the railway crossing north of the old station to the river bridge and on to Oakdale.

21. Snow blocking the southern entrance to the town in 1947. The Parrot advertises Buchan's Rhymney Beers. Austin Morgan (grocer) and Morris the Beehive are opposite.

22. A general view of the Factory Lane area adjacent to the Sirhowy river. In the near right foreground is the old pump house behind which are the 'Gossy' steps. The field has become Sunningdale Nurseries. The river flows diagonally across the upper part of the picture. Behind it is Glanyrafon Park, the home of Blackwood RFC, and the gas holder beyond that.

CHAPTER 2

The Surrounding Villages

23. Looking south towards the shops in Maindee Road, Cwmfelinfach in 1960.

24. The main bridge over the Sirhowy river at Ynysddu in 1905.

25. Morrisville, between Cwmfelinfach and Wattsville c1950. The road in the picture leads to Brynawel.

26. The Welfare Grounds between Cwmfelinfach and Ynysddu in the 1950s, showing the well kept tennis courts and bowling green.

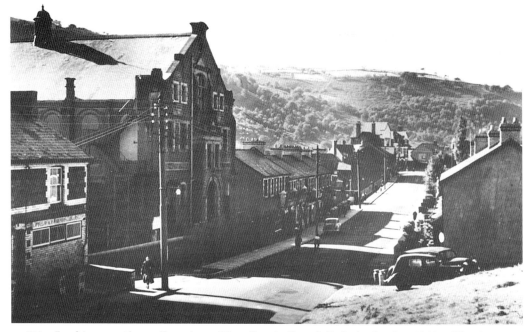

27. Looking up the valley along New Road, Cwmfelinfach, in the 1940s. The large building on the left is the Workmen's Institute, which was destroyed by fire in 1996. To the left is the Cwmfelinfach Workmen's Club and Institute. Note the three milk churns to the rear of the parked cars. This was the time when milk was sold from small churns and dispensed directly into the householder's jug. It cost 4^{1}/2d a pint, less than the equivalent of 2p today.

28. A general view of Ynysddu from the west taken c1905. The problem of building a house on the side of a mountain is solved by building houses that appeared 3-storey from one side and 2-storey from the other. At this time the main road through the valley was along the upper street in this photograph. Subsequently a new main road was constructed near the course of the river.

29. This photograph of the northern half of Wyllie Village was taken from the old Newport Road on the other side of the valley. The straight line at the bottom is the 'new' road from Pontllanfraith to Ynysddu, and the horizontal line, almost half way up, shows the line of the Tredegar to Newport railway. Closed many years ago, this line is now part of the Sirhowy Valley Walk.

30. Glanhowy Road, Wyllie, pre-1939. Trees have been planted along the pavement and stand in the company of some most elaborate street lamps. Note the well cared for privet hedges.

31. The Village Institute, Wyllie, built in 1934, and shown here soon after the Second World War. For the last decade the building has experienced a change of use - it is now the Islwyn Inn.

32. The Mill, Gelligroes, taken from the south looking towards Pontllanfraith. Four ancient paths meet here in the form of two separate north-south routes, one on either side of the Sirhowy river. They are linked by an old stone bridge set to the right of the mill.

33. The Old Mill, Gelligroes, taken in 1970. The twelve foot diameter wheel, some six feet wide, turned twelve times a minute under the mill race which was fed by water from the Sirhowy. Clever gearing turned the two pairs of four feet millstones one hundred and forty times a minute. Part of the water power was used to generate electricity which was used to light the mill, the mill house (shown here to the left) and to charge batteries for cars and radios before World War I. The farmer at Ty Llwyd Farm, Ynysddu, was one of the first to establish radio contact with the Moore brothers at the mill - he used to radio in his orders. It is also recorded that radio messages from the Titanic at the time of its sinking were received here. In recent years the mill has become associated with top quality candle making. David Constable uses the old stable block as a factory and lives in Mill House. The old mill is open as a museum.

34. This War Memorial was originally erected in front of the Mynyddislwyn Council Offices opposite the railway level-crossing in Pontllanfraith but now stands in the grounds of the former Islwyn Borough Council Offices near Pontllanfraith Comprehensive School.

35. The names of those men from the Pontllanfraith area who lost their lives serving King and Country during the two World Wars 1914-18 and 1939-45.

Roll of Honour - Pontllanfraith 1914-18 War

C Allock	J Humphries	A Price
S Bethel	B Jefferies	E Price
J Bryant	E W Jenkins	S Price
R Bull	R Jenkins	D E Rees
T Coles	A V Jennings	Ll Richards
E D Cook	E H Jennings	A Richardson
H T Crabtree	H Jennings	J Richardson
A Cripps	D J Jones	D Roberts
Ed Cripps	F J Jones	E Roberts
E Cripps	I Jones	H Roberts
D Davies	T Jones	S Roberts
D T W Davies	W Lewis	J Rogers
G Davies	A T Lloyd	W Rogers
L Davies	T Lockwood	N Saunders
T J Davies	E Mansfield	R Travers
W Davies	J McDougall	H Tucker
A Dowden	C W C Myles	H T Walding
G Evans	G Powles	D Walters
E Gingell	R Powles	A Williams
F J Hale	J Preston	T D Williams

Roll of Honour - Pontllanfraith 1939-45 War

A J Blakeman	B Jones	V C Rutland
N Burrows	P K Jones	C Sewell
L Cardwell	V Jones	F R Sibley
L C Daniels	W F Lloyd	J E Thomas
C Davies	E Meredith	J Walters
J C Davies	W Osland	I W Watkins
E Evans	W R Pearce	A N Williams
T Evans	G E Peck	L Williams
J S Elias	R Pugh	M L Woodley
E Harwood	C C Reed	
F C Hawkins	P J Rees	

36. Pontllanfraith from a spot near St Augustine's Church during the first decade of the century. The school (top left) was destroyed by fire in 1911. Two people sit in a horse and trap outside the Greyhound Hotel. The unused space to the right of the hotel will be the site for S D Roberts & Co automobile engineers and Ford dealers when the age of the motorcar arrives. This business was later operated by Gibbs Bros.

37. The Open Air Swimming Baths at Pontllanfraith, opened just prior to World War Two. This photograph, taken soon after the war, shows houses which had been built in a completely new way. Much of the building was prefabricated in factories and simply assembled on site.

38. The Penllwyn Inn, Pontllanfraith. Formerly Penllwyn Sarf, meaning 'top of the bushes of the serpent', this was the chief seat of Edmund Morgan, grandson of Sir John Morgan, who had fought on the side of Henry VII. Built after the Battle of Bosworth, which ended The War of the Roses, this 16th century stone tiled two-storey Tudor mansion with square headed windows is in an excellent position on high ground overlooking the Sirhowy river.

39. Vehicles wait for the level crossing to open at Pontllanfraith top station in the early 1950s. To the left the War Memorial stands in front of the Mynyddislwyn U D C offices. Mynyddislwyn U D C was formed on 29 September 1903 and had been divided into four wards by 1910. The memorial was removed from here to the grounds of the newly formed Islwyn Borough Council Offices when the councils of Bedwellty and Mynyddislwyn, together with Abercarn and Risca, were merged.

40. This old, badly worn photograph, taken c1900, shows five men standing around a combined finger post/street lamp. The right hand finger points to Blackwood, the left hand one to New Tredegar and the finger in the centre to Aberbargoed. This post was about half way between the New Inn, Bedwellty and Bedwellty Church. It was around this spot that one of the earliest communities in the area evolved. Apart from the New Inn and St Sannan's Church, there was the Church Inn and one of our earliest schools. As the parish became industrialised the importance of the parish church and the area immediately surrounding it diminished. New Tredegar, Aberbargoed and, in particular, Blackwood, became the centres of business and commerce.

41. The New Inn, Bedwellty as it was during the first part of the century. The licensee was S Challenger. Note the stone tiles on the roof. During major restoration the lean-to building at the end was demolished, two of the doorways were blocked up, new windows installed, and the furthest house was incorporated into the New Inn as a restaurant. This well run old pub was tastefully refurbished under the watchful eye of 'Sam' Takla, the licensee, and his wife Sue who looks after the catering.

42. Looking north along Bedwellty Road, Cefn Fforest in the late 1930s. There is an advertisment for the Regal cinema, Fleur-de-lys on the end wall of the house. (The Regal cinema site is now occupied by a Health Centre). The corner building to the right is the Midland Bank, formerly the London Joint City & Midland Bank, later to become Cefn Fforest Police Station and subsequently a doctor's surgery.

43. 'The schools' at Cefn Fforest, Blackwood, in the early 1920s having been opened on 18 October 1915. The first headteacher was Mr John T Watkins who, together with four teachers, was responsible for the education of 338 pupils ranging from 5 to 13+. Some teachers!! An entry in the school log for May 1926 is particularly revealing about local conditions: Attendance is dwindling rapidly as the General Strike hits the country and is affecting the children as well. Many children are needed to forage for coal and to help at home during this tragic time. The school is used to provide midday meals for needy children.

44. A scene at Oakdale near the entrance to Penrhiwbengi Lane and looking along Syr Dafydd Avenue during the early years of World War Two. The Post Office and shops are on the right, Rhiw Syr Dafydd straight ahead in the distance, while Penmaen Avenue leads, on the left, to the centre of the village.

45. An old postcard showing Ty Melin (Mill House), Argoed. This was the site for Oakdale colliery which was opened in 1908. The colliery closed in 1989 and the site has now been cleared completely, possibly to be developed as an industrial estate.

46. This pre-World War Two photograph shows Rhiw Syr Dafydd and Oakdale colliery on the right and the fields of Cwm Gelli farm, Blackwood, on the left. The scene is predominantly rural and is little changed today apart from the disappearance of the colliery.

47. Llwyn Onn Road, Oakdale, pre 1920. The trees of this modern mining village are still relatively young. An unwashed miner on his way home poses near a street lamp. In the foreground railway lines stop abruptly.

48. A very smart Auntie Marie and George stand proudly outside their relatively new home: 5 Beech Grove, Oakdale in September 1916. This photograph shows quality housing almost unheard of for miners then. Each house had a large coal-burning range with an open fire, side oven and back boiler. Constant hot water was 'on tap' and this, together with a separate bathroom, represented paradise for the average miner's family of the time. The intention had been that every home also had electricity from the colliery but a dispute at the time of installation prevented this happening except for part of Syr Dafydd Avenue and the officials' houses in Penrhiw Terrace. The other homes in the village had to manage on oil lamps and candles until they were connected to the gas supply. Electricity arrived eventually in the 1930s.

49. Looking towards Oakdale colliery and village in the early 1950s. Argoed High Street, comprising shops, Post Office (opened in 1908), the Baptist Chapel and the Argoed Arms hotel, is shown in the foreground. An Act of Parliament, dated 25 May 1860, resulted in the Sirhowy Tramroad, which ran through High Street, being renamed the Sirhowy Railway and being re-routed on the eastern side of the shops and houses. At the same time the gauge of the track became standard.

50. The Square in Oakdale, looking south along Central Avenue, before the development of the open central area. There is just one car; how different is the same scene today.

51. Looking along Central Avenue on a sunny spring day in the late 1940s. A Saxon lorry delivers pop while a baker returns to his van.

52. Some very stray woods are in evidence in this relaxing 1940s summer's day scene at Oakdale Bowling Green.

53. Young bathers with their dogs at Pen-y-fan pond in the early part of the century. It was a long way to the sea, and in those days finding convenient transport was difficult and expensive. This pond provided an adequate substitute and was very popular with locals.

54. Looking across from Penylan, Argoed, towards Oakdale Colliery. This was before the Argoed - Tredegar road was improved. It shows the Sirhowy river, Cwm Argoed in the centre, and the railway and its buildings to the right.

55. A picture of the old river bridge Argoed, taken between the wars.

56. A pre-war general view of Argoed from the east showing the road from the 'old' main street to Penylan. An engine pulls a long line of trucks filled with coal, above which is the school. The original Public Elementary School (mixed and infants) was built in 1899 for 250 children, and was enlarged in 1906 to accommodate 220 mixed and 99 infants. Llwynfedw, the large house in the centre, set in its own grounds, belonged to the local doctor; first Dr Reynolds and afterwards Dr Edward J Jones. It was from here that Dr Jones in partnership with Dr T J Davies operated their medical practice. As this was more than two miles from the nearest chemist they were obliged to dispense medicines. This they did in the adjacent pharmacy.

57. Cwm Corrwg, Argoed, known locally as Cwm Argoed. The picture shows Sir Thomas Phillips' school, together with the bell housing, in the upper left hand corner of the photograph. The school was erected in 1842 to accommodate 300 children at a cost of £1400, half of which was contributed by Sir Thomas. His colliery workmen were required to pay 1d in the £ of their earnings to the school, in return for which their children were educated free. An adult school was open two evenings a week. In 1844 there were 136 pupils on the books producing an average attendance of 124. Church services were held in the school until the opening of Court y bella Church in 1857.

58. Cwm Corrwg, Argoed, looking east over the Castle Hotel from the main Blackwood-Tredegar road near Sunnyview. The local shop can be seen through the trees on the right. The path running diagonally across this scene leads from the village to the railway line. At river level there were two mill wheels, one for corn and the other for a flannel factory. This was the only place in Monmouthshire where two mill wheels turned within 30 yards of each other. Major repairs were carried out on the mills in 1848 and 1869 by Gwillim Jenkins, mason.

59. The stone viaduct at Abernant-y-felin, Argoed. This viaduct still exists but has been almost totally obliterated by colliery waste which has been tipped along both sides of the arches. The tops of the arches are still visible from the main Blackwood-Tredegar road near Manmoel Crossing.

60. A general view of Argoed from the south east in the 1930s. The prosperous looking white building in the centre is the Castle Hotel, above which is the Baptist Chapel and the stationmaster's house. Note the spoil tip high up on the left and the school on the right.

61. The corner position of the Post Office, Pengam, Mon, and its adjacent house, in 1910. Opposite was the school dental clinic where so many children in the 1940s and 50s suffered teeth extractions under gas.

62. The view from the river bridge between Pengam and Fleur-de-lys in 1921. Lewis' School Pengam stands on the skyline with Cardiff Road on the left.

63. Neuaddwen Farm, on the eastern side of Aberbargoed high up on the road to Bedwellty Church. Two women attend to the needs of the cows in the yard while a mother and child stand with others on the road outside. This farm became the Neuadd Wen Inn more than thirty years ago, but today is known as The Farm.

64. This photograph shows the Powell Duffryn Workmen's Hospital, Aberbargoed soon after it was opened in 1909. It was built at a cost, including equipment, of £6000 and was for the benefit of the workpeople in the Rhymney Valley who were employed by the Powell Duffryn Steam Coal Company. It could accommodate 24 patients and was supported by contributions from the workforce.

65. The Memorial Gates, Aberbargoed, erected in the 1920s to commemorate the young men of the town who had given their lives in The Great War. The workmen's hospital stands behind.

66. The view from Bargoed looking towards Bedwellty Church early in the century. Bargoed Colliery stands in the foreground with the town of Aberbargoed on the opposite side of the valley.

67. It is quite unusual for this area of the United Kingdom to experience deep snow. This scene shows the principal exception in living memory. A team of men are removing snow on the road from Bedwellty Church to Cefn Fforest in the winter of 1947. The figure in the foreground is carrying fuel.

68. A general view c1935 of Markham village and its colliery. The name Markham derives from Sir Arthur Markham, the owner of the colliery, who was born in Chesterfield in 1866. His maternal grandfather, Sir Joseph Paxton, was the designer of the 1851 Hyde Park Industrial Exhibition and was in charge of the erection of the Crystal Palace, London. Sir Arthur's early working life involved numerous engineering and colliery enterprises. He was always keen to be involved with the latest technology and pioneered the use of electricity in the mines of South Wales beginning with Markham and Oakdale. He was also instrumental in planning the model villages near these two collieries. In 1910 he entered parliament as the Liberal MP for Mansfield, Nottinghamshire where he remained until he was created a baronet in 1911. He died in 1916 still, by today's standards, a relatively young man.

69. Traffic problems between Markham Baths and Hollybush during the winter of 1973.

70. This photograph, taken from the south in the 1920s, shows the village of Hollybush straddled along the main Blackwood-Tredegar road. It shows Llwyn Arfon Farm high up the slopes on the left and the school at the northern end of the village.

CHAPTER 3

Religion & Education

71. The ancient chapel at Manmoel in the 1920s.

72. The Mission Church, Ynysddu, soon after it was opened in 1905. This building, which could seat 350 people, was used as the Church Hall as soon as St Theodore's was built in 1925. It was lost in a fire about a decade ago.

73. Babell Chapel, Cwmfelinfach. This chapel, built in 1827, is the last resting place of the Rev. William Thomas, a Calvinistic Methodist minister, better known by his bardic title Islwyn. Islwyn was one of the finest nineteenth century poets that Wales produced.

74. The Methodist Church, Wyllie, in the early 1930s. It was modelled on the mother church in Blackwood which had been opened on St. David's Day 1928. Sadly, a decline in peoples' interest in religion forced this church to close and fall into a state of decay. It was taken down some years ago.

75. St Tudor's Church, Mynyddislwyn, from the south west as it appeared c1910. A spacious church in Early English style, it consists of a chancel, nave, aisles, south porch and embattled tower with three bells. It was rebuilt in 1820 with seating for 550 and there is clear evidence that all the outside walls, including the tower, were, for long periods, white washed. The parish register dates from 1664.

76. The impressive modern stained glass window in blues and yellows, in the nave of St. Tudor's Church. Given by the Gibbs family it was designed and made by John Petts of Llanstephan. Much controversy has recently surrounded another John Petts window which he designed for St. Mary's Church, Cardiff.

77. St Tudor's Church, Mynyddislwyn from the north west. The Church Inn stands to the left and the tumulus known as Twyn Tudor is to the right of the church.

78. The Calvinistic Methodist Chapel at Gelligroes. Built in the nineteenth century and still going strong, part of this building was used as a school.

79. St. Sannan's, the parish church of Bedwellty, from the south. The church, built in Early English style, consists of a chancel, nave, north aisle, south porch and embattled western tower with six bells. This photograph was taken c1900. The organ was presented by Evan Thomas of Builth in memory of his wife. Around this time the churchyard was extended to five acres but has been increased further at least twice since. Bedwellty parish stretched from Tredegar in the north to Blackwood in the south, and from Rhymney and Pengam in the east to Ebbw Vale in the west, an area of more that 7000 acres. Parish registers date from 1624.

80. This photograph, taken in the chancel of Bedwellty Church, clearly shows 'mason marks' which can be seen arrowed in the centre, to the left and right. The precise meaning of these marks is uncertain. Some say that they were to show the position of a stone in the structure; others that they showed which mason had cut a particular stone and thus could indicate a way in which payment could be determined.

81. The base of one of the piers separating the nave from the north aisle in Bedwellty Church. For a long period the level of the floor was much higher than it is today. The erosion visible is due to water.

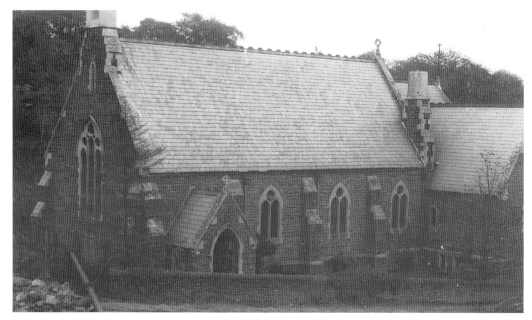

82. St. Margaret's Church, Blackwood from the south west in 1920. The church is dedicated to St. Margaret of Antioch who lived at the time of the emperor Diocletian and was martyred c310. It is said that she was thrown into prison for refusing the advances of one of the Governors. Whilst there she was visited by the devil in the form of a dragon which she repelled. She never lost her faith and eventually was beheaded. Her feast day is 20th July.

83. Choristers who took part in a Singing Festival at The Central Methodist Church, Blackwood on 25 May 1983 with Mr Gordon Bennett their conductor. Back row: Elsie Lewis, Mrs White, Miss Harris, Len Jones, Gwyn Thomas, Glyn Morgan, Jeffrey Ellis, Ray Holding, Ken Davies, Trevor Trace. Third row: Betty Price, Enid Davies, Myrtle Jones, Shirley Watkins, Kath Coleman, Hilda Morgan, Eunice Powell, Mary Morgan, Molly James, Dilys Powell. Second row: Margaret Evans, unknown, Alice Bennett, Mary Brown, Alma Bennett, Blanche Thomas, Marjorie Holding. Front row: Ieuan Wyn Jones JP, Harry Riley, Mr Thomas, Arthur Coleman, Geraldus Evans. The organist is Hadyn Panes.

84. This photograph, taken in 1925 in the grounds of Beaumont House, Bloomfield Road, shows Past and Present Teachers and Officers of Mount Pleasant Baptist Sunday School, Cefn Road, Blackwood. Back Row: Mrs W. Carey, Miss E F Reeves, Mr A Brown, Mr Richard Smith, Secretary 1933-34, Mr Victor Norman, Secretary 1939-41, Organist 1937-1965, Mr Edwin Jones (Tirfilkins Farm). Standing, Fourth Row: Mr. H J Lewis (Jnr), Mr Ewart Smith, Secretary 1929-33, Mr H J Lewis (Snr), Mr C Williams. Standing, Third Row: Mr Joseph Harris, Mrs Chas Vaughan, Mrs B Morgan, Mrs Powling, Mrs W O Williams, Miss Stokes, Miss Budding, Mrs Veater, Miss E Gibbs, Mr Alfred Richards, Treasurer 1931-1948. Seated: Mrs. Edith Smith, Mr Thomas Norman, Mr George Reeves, Treasurer 1915-1918, Mr Isaac Harrhy, Sunday School Superintendent, Mr Charles Vaughan, Treasurer pre. 1909, Mr James Morgan, Rev. W O Williams (minister from September 1915 to October 1940), Mrs Evans (Beaumont House). In Front: Mr. J. Aubrey, Miss E Harris, Mrs Olive Lewis, Mrs Hilda Morgan, Miss Hilda Richards, Mr. T J Morgan.

85. The monument to James Thomas (1817 - 1901) of Ty Newydd, Porth at New Bethel Chapel, Mynyddislwyn. New Bethel was originally built in 1765 but rebuilt in 1855.

86. Miss Tilley Hamer (later Mrs Evans) with her class at Blackwood Elementary School on 5 November 1946. Mr Dick Lewis the headmaster, stands on the left. Back row: Margaret Stevens, unknown, Lena Thomas, Nancy May, unknown, unknown, J Bishop, unknown, Audrey Chivers, unknown. Middle row: Mr D Lewis, Audrey King, unknown, Elizabeth Parker, Gwyneth Price, Margaret Baker, Mrs T Hamer, unknown, Rosemary Perkins, unknown, Mary Butterworth, Jean Gwilt. Seated: unknown, Letty Southgate, Jean Gibbs, unknown, Jill Parker, J Tapper, Sheila Williams, June Gould, unknown, Molly Seymour.

87. The Education Act of 1870 resulted in the newly formed Bedwellty School Board appointing Jane Annie James on 13 August 1873 as the teacher for the new school which was to function at The Drill Hall, Blackwood. The opening of the school was publicised in the chapels and opened to pupils on 8 September. 65 pupils registered. When they returned to start school on the following Monday 73 boys and girls were admitted. Only 15 could read monosyllables, and only one could work sums in simple multiplication. Some of the entries in the school log book are listed below.

10 Oct. 1873 Called at Red Lion Inn to ask if Catherine Williams would become a monitor. She started as a trial monitor on 13 October.

15 Oct. Considerable interruption - people preparing for a function in the Drill Hall in the evening.

24 Oct. Rev. Theophilus visited the school. Catherine Williams monitor is to receive 2/6 (12$^1/_2$ p) a week. When appointed, a pupil teacher is to be paid £8 p.a to start, rising to £10 if satisfactory.

6 Nov. Blackboards, easels and cupboards arrived to go with eleven desks that arrived last week

13 Nov. Mr. Morris (he was in business where Tidal's Stores is today) to give the children a holiday today so that the Drill Hall can be decorated for a concert in aid of a new church.

15 Nov. Mrs. Sheppan had received her money for cleaning before properly earning it. In future Mistress must initial that her work has been properly done.

10 Dec. Expelled Elizabeth Casnett (13 yrs) for beating Catherine Williams, the monitor. (They had their problems then!)

2 Feb. 1874 Jerusalem School opened today - has not affected numbers here.

5 Feb. Dismissed Samuel Jenkins (14 yrs) for insubordination

25 Feb. School closed p.m. - preparation for Volunteers Dinner. (The Volunteers were a military organisation that had been formed in the early part of the century to defend the country. The Volunteers could be called up at short notice and sent abroad.)

26 Feb. When I got to school - room not ready, no fire, children had been drinking beer, wine and spirits left over from previous night.

23 Mar. 11 new scholars - have now reached 189 since opening.

1 June Think it better to close in future during Whitsun week instead of Easter, as picnics keep pupils away.

26 June Closed school for 4 weeks (This was the school summer holiday)

28 August Measles spreading. I sent away my relations to avoid infection.

21 Sept. Only Jane James can keep order in school. Friction between Jane James and the Sergeant of the Volunteers - he had told the children that there was no school.

28 Sept. Mr. Morris came at 3 p.m. He requested me to close the school at once, at the same time other members of the corps arrived. Mr. Morris stated that the adjutant would be present in 20 minutes and expressed his surprise that I had not given the children a half-day, saying that the children knew it (things haven't changed - children always know what is happening long before the teachers!!) and a notice was in the window telling the Volunteers to meet him here today. I told him I never notice notices in the window believing that they concern the Volunteers and not me, and unless I received a proper message on the subject I would never close the school. I then dismissed the school as quickly as possible and was at home when the train passed bringing the adjutant.

23 Oct. Half-day holiday for two funerals of scholars. Lilly Watkins and Julia Harry (Jane James' niece), both aged between 4 and 5 buried today. All teachers and many pupils attended the one of Julia Harry. The two funerals started in company as far as the corner of Saddlers Lane (the present day Square), one taking the road to Penmaen Chapel - the other to Bedwellty Church.

28 Oct. Drill Hall whitewashed (inside). No notice given by Mr. Morris. Very wet, pupils sent home. People do not like being treated like this - they are now paying 3d (1p) for 3 days schooling.

1 Dec. another death in school - Julia Theating

16 Dec. Deep fall of snow

2 Feb. 1875 Sarah Jenkins away - wholly unfit for a teacher. Idle, sleepy and obliged to oblige her numerous relations.

8 Feb. Went to Newport to get a tooth and old stump extracted by dentist.

14 April Carpenters put a latch on the girls' back door low enough for the infants to reach. They had often been shut out in the rain.

16 August The foundation stone of Blackwood Church (St Margaret's) laid today and Drill Hall required as a robing room for the Bishop and clergy

29 Sept. Photograph of children taken.

11 Oct. Readmitted two girls aged 8 and 10. Mother said they do not learn anything at Jerusalem School.

22 Oct. The clock has now been stopped for 16 months.

26 Oct. Mr. Morris called to measure for a curtain to go over the large doors. Still no suitable lavatory seat for infants children.

January 1876 Government Report. This school, which has been conducted for the last two years in temporary and very inconvenient premises, has passed on the whole a satisfactory examination. The reading is decidedly good and the writing and spelling are also good - or fairly good in the three lower standards, above which no scholars were presented. Arithmetic which is but fair or pretty fair in the first and second standards is almost a complete failure in the third standard. This subject will need attention. The Infants' Instruction has been on the whole well attended to. Grant claimed £52.2.0

11 Oct. HMI called - the children appear quite stupid before a stranger, even those who generally do well.

27 Oct. Children now appear to attend as well on a Friday as a Monday.

30 Sept. Closed school 10 mins early. Too dark to do anything. (A pointed reminder of what things were like before the advent of electricity.)

5 Dec. Mrs. Evans called - I had refused to allow her big boy to bring his dinner because he lives near the school and only comes to make a noise and give the teachers trouble.

11 Dec. Lewis Lewis - worse for drink. I passed him on the way to school. Using indecent language - not fit for the girls to hear.

18 Dec. Gave holiday last Friday to attend Police Court re. Lewis Lewis. He admitted his error and was bound over to keep the peace. (The law moved a little faster in those days!!)

27 April 1877 Attended a Committee Meeting at new school. Tea to be given to children at the opening. (This was the school on Cefn Road next to where Mount Pleasant chapel now stands. It served the children of the town until it was closed on 22 October 1980, when the pupils were moved to Apollo Way.)

3 May New school opened by Mr Laybourne. 178 children moved from the Drill Hall starting at about 12 noon. The key was handed by the architect to the Chairman of the Board to the Chairman of the Committee and on to me (the headmistress).

28 May Started Infants School

88. Mrs. Pat Jenkins with her class at Cefn Road Infants' School in the early 1980s.

89. St. David's Day at Blackwood Infants School in 1988. Standing: Amanda Love, Lianne Davies, Lisa Butler, Rachel Taylor, Claire Vickers, Joanne Powell, Kathy Bettany, Rachel Carey. In front: Kelly Birch, Connie Edmunds, Tamara Dowler, Jackie Lawson, Caroline Williams.

90. Girl Prefects at Pontllanfraith Grammar School, 1950-51. Standing: Hazel Cummings, Molly Maquire, Helen White, Pam Saunders, Tracey Winterson, Avril Hughes, Shirley Gwilt, Jean Hambleton. Seated: Maureen Hunt, Ivy Jones, Mr Cliff Rowlands (headmaster) Pam Houghton, unknown.

91. An unusual sight for 1951 - a boys' Cookery Competition at Pontllanfraith Grammar School.

92. Mrs Julie Silcocks with Class 2 at Markham Primary School in 1993. The headmaster is Mr J C Holly. Back row John Postians, Lee Burton, John Powell, Kaine Stevens, Wayne Edwards, Lee Davies, Lee Rawle, Paul Watkins, Gerard O'Connell. Third row: Samantha Chamberlain, Sarah Bendle, Sarah Jones, Cara Postians, Sarah Coonick, Nadine Finn, Stuart Vokes. Second row: Ceri Howells, Carly Baker, Emma Davies, Hannah Lee, Rachel Jones, Leanne Conway, Sarah Finlayson. Front row: Christopher Rock, Craig Ingram, David Waite, Gavin Jones, John Purnell, Nathan Davies, Lewis Hughes.

93. Markham Primary School's Welsh Folk Dancing Team which competed at Cwmbran on 18 June 1994. Back row: Katy A'Hearne, Lyn Coonick, Helen Lancaster, Katie Williams, Clair Craddock, Donna Morgan, Natalie Heron, Samantha Williams, Kirsty Strip, Gavin Edwards, Rhys Powell, Andrew Robinson. Front row: Lewis Hughes, Thomas Davies, Lisa Rawle, Carly Baker, Erica Taylor, Hollie Thomas, Rhiannon Howells, Stacey Powell, Kayleigh A'Hearne, Martin Jones.

94. Apollo Way Infants' School, March 1985. A representative of the NSPCC is receiving a cheque for £1,100 from two of the pupils.

95. An early photograph showing 51 Standard II pupils at Ynysddu Infants' School. Let's hope that the two adults are both Standard II teachers and that it's not the headmistress with one teacher who has a class of 51!

96. Blackwood School soon after the end of World War Two. Pupils moved to this school from the Infants' School on Cefn Road and most of them stayed here until they completed their education. Since the advent of Blackwood Secondary Modern School (now Blackwood Comprehensive School) this school has been used as Blackwood Mixed Junior School educating children from the age of eight until they proceeded to secondary school.

97. Miss Joan Maiden (right), the Headmistress, and Mrs Marion Evans with her class at Blackwood Infants' School in 1970.

98. Class 4A, Pontllanfraith Junior School, 1965-1966 with their teacher Mr John Coker. Back row: Marilyn Roberts, Lynne Ralph, Ruth Bater, Sonia Parfitt, Melita Hoskins, Alun Davies, Alwyn Williams, Colin Harris, David Stephens. Third row: Gay Dudley, Christina Butler, Keith Woodley, Susanne Salter, Christine Matthews, Carol Trace, Paul Jenkins, Ross Davies, Patricia Fears. Second row: Giannina Marruzzi, Sandra Childs, Wayne Nowaczyk, Beverley Waite, Jayne Windsor, Carol Hoare, Lynnette Cook, Eric Hughes, David Rogers. Front row: Julia Thomas, Jayne Brown, Ann Plummer, Hilary Davies, Gail Rawlings, Pamela Stephens. Giannina Marruzzi is the daughter of the owners of the cafe that used to stand opposite the Lower Station at Pontllanfraith. When her parents retired she returned to Italy with them, became a linguist, and now lectures at an Italian University. Wayne Nowaczyk is the son of a Polish miner who settled in Pontllanfraith after the war. Wayne is a reporter for the South Wales Echo.

99. The staff and pupils of Pontllanfraith Grammar School in 1928. The Headmaster is Mr E C Bowen. Mr C Rowlands the next headmaster, is sitting three seats from Mr Bowen on the left.

100. Miss Pett's class at Fairview Elementary School c1930. Back row: Billy Smith, unknown, Jack Hamer, Mable Peters, unknown, unknown, Jimmy Woods, Sylvia Poulton, Garfield Hemmings. Third row: Jackie Pugh, Zena Williams, Graham Davies, Tommy May, Joyce Vale, Betty Rowlands, Marcel Pleasance, Flossie Smith, Elsie Warnel, and unknown. Second row: Clifford Cook, Pearl Thurlow, A Main, Susie Whitehouse, unknown, Gwen Jones, Raymond Lewis, Muriel Beddis, Ray Taylor, unknown and Evan Morgan. Front row: Freddie Clease, unknown, Lionel Evans, unknown, Charlie Smith, unknown, Benny Brown, unknown, A Charles, unknown, B Charles and Tommy Rees.

101. Miss Jenny Jones' class at Blackwood Elementary School in 1942. Back row: unknown, Joan Daniels, Billy Bickley, Gary Rosser, Gordon Leach, Keith Mudford, Clifford Davies, Gordon King and unknown. Third row: Miss Jenny Jones, unknown, Lal Holvey, June Bennett, Doris Whitney, Pam Miles, Beryl Meek, Margaret Baker, Margaret Amesbury and Mr Dick Lewis (Headmaster). Seated: Unknown, Jean Watkins, Doris Stokes, Sylvia Hazel, Rosenna Watkins, Kathleen Lewis, Beryl Lewis, Jeanette Morgan, Enid Griffiths, Barbara Taylor and Jean Withey. Front row: Dennis Williams, Derek Burrows, Fred Sarah, Graydon Oakley and unknown.

102. Class 1, Blackwood Junior School, with their teacher, Mrs Daphne Lewis, in 1976. Back row: Stephen Baker, Gareth Davies, Jonathan Smith, Ian Carey, Noel Chard, Andrew Clements, Damien Rogers, Colin Jones. Middle row: Martin Cullen, Sheri Withey, unknown, Karen Jones, Nicola Summerill, unknown, David Joseph. Seated: Ellen Huckle, Nicola Berkley, Tracey Mullins, Suzanne Lewis, Tracy Rowlands, Denine Burton, Emma Jane Brown.

103. Sir Thomas Phillips, QC (1801-1867) was born at Ynysgarth, Clydach in the parish of Llanelly, Powys. He moved with his parents to Trosnant, Pontypool, and later became a solicitor in Newport. Sir Thomas was a prominent colliery owner in Gwent, owning collieries at Manmoel and Court y bella. He dominated the education scene in Wales during the years 1820-60. In 1842 he was responsible for establishing the first school in this area, namely Courtybella Colliery School, a few miles up the valley from Blackwood on the Mynyddislwyn side of the Sirhowy river. In 1838 he became Mayor of Newport and played a significant part in quashing the Chartist outbreak of 1839. His success resulted in an invitation to stay with Queen Victoria at Windsor Castle from whom he subsequently received a knighthood.

104. Pupils from Fairview Elementary School in 1946 with cups and a shield which they had won when they swept the board in the Area Sports' Day. Back row: Phillys Barret, Zena Morgan, Jean Clark, Jean Pullen, Mrs Brockett, Gwerfyl Jones, Miriam Brown, Mr Evans, Muriel Pearce, Ray Barret, Jimmy Cordell. Seated: Gwyneth Jones, Norman Smith, Ray Smith, Cliff Tombes, N Thomas, Barbara Williams, Terry Flowers, Lyndon Bartlett, Doris Perkins, unknown. In front: G Padfield, G Anthony, Pat Norman, unknown, John Cordell, Morgan Healy, Phillip Williams, Ronald Trace, unknown.

105. A teacher, monitors and pupils at Blackwood Mixed School, Cefn Road, c1903. The school was opened by Mr Laybourne on 3 May 1877 and closed on 22 October 1980. Many older inhabitants will recall the name of the headmistress, Miss M E Major. She was appointed head in 1910 and was still there in 1939. Cefn Court was built on the site soon after the school closed.

106. Pontllanfraith Comprehensive School's Parents' Association in 1976. The Headmaster, Mr E Maguire, stands on the left.

107. The Sunday School with their teachers at the Central Methodist Church, Blackwood, in 1974. Mrs Mary Morgan J P stands on the left.

108. Mrs Marion Evans with her Sunday School pupils at the Central Methodist Church in 1974.

CHAPTER 4

Trade, Industry & Transport

TOTAL LENGTH - 1142' 0"

RHYMNEY
TRAVELLER'S REST
BEERS

Bedwellty Road Aberbargoed

109. Bird's eye view of the hill, with the bus coming down about to make two awkward turns and pass under the railway bridge. There were at least seven public houses located on the hill, but apart from the Duffryn Arms at the top (which was later converted into the Bedwellty Council Offices) not one was a bus stop, request or otherwise.

West Monmouthshire Omnibus Board

The valleys of West Monmouthshire, which are geologically and geographically similar to those of Glamorganshire, developed rapidly in the nineteenth century as important colliery areas. The local transport system was based on the railway, the most important need being to take advantage of the gradients to haul coal to the most expedient port. While the railways provided a transport system up and down the valleys it fell to the lot of the motor bus to provide a public service between one deep valley and the next. Bedwellty Urban District Council, in whose area Blackwood was the principal town, promoted a Bill in the 1920s to create and operate a local bus company but the opposition of Lewis & James, the largest private bus company, succeeded in defeating the Bill in the committee stage. Soon after the Mynyddislwyn Urban District Council decided to promote a similar Bill and Bedwellty UDC, realising that it held Blackwood, the commercial centre of the combined areas, joined forces with Mynyddislwyn to form the West Monmouthshire Omnibus Board. The necessary Act of Parliament received the Royal Assent on 4 August 1926. The two councils removed any opposition to their proposals by buying out all the local routes belonging to Lewis & James, the Griffin Motor Co. and Valley Motor Bus Services that had starting and terminal points within the urban districts of Bedwellty and Mynyddislwyn. These were the early days of public and passenger transport. It was a turbulent competitive period when the local authorities were the statutory licensing authorities of stage carriage services. This situation was changed by the 1930 Road Traffic Act which placed all statutory control in the hands of the Regional Traffic Commissioners whose strict and rigid regime lasted until Deregulation in 1986. West Mon, as it was locally known, held a special place within the 96 local authority undertakings. Firstly, unlike other municipal undertakings it operated under a private Act of Parliament, and secondly its service between Bargoed and Aberbargoed operated on one of the most severe routes anywhere in the country. The bus first travelled along a narrow, winding road out of Bargoed, then turned right to climb the hill. The road passed under a very low railway bridge, turned at right angles as soon as it reached the far side, followed almost immediately by another right angle turn, this time to the left. Apart from these two corners the road was straight but very steep. After the bridge the gradient was 1 in $4^{3}/_{4}$ for 225 feet, followed by 500 ft at 1 in 5 or 1 in 6 and then a stretch at 1 in 10 before easing off at 1 in 13 towards the top. The turn under the bridge was extremely difficult, particularly for a bus coming down the hill. The driver had to turn sharp right on the first bend and then almost immediately swing over to full left lock in order to clear the bridge. The turn on to left lock had to be made at a critical point within about 12 inches, otherwise the nearside of the bus would catch the left-hand arch of the bridge and the offside front corner would catch the right-hand side. The service operated on this hill from 1927 until 1964, originally with Saurer, then with Leyland Bulls and finally with Leyland Titan buses. All these buses were fitted with sprag gearing which prevented them running backwards. Because of the arduous nature of the route it was worked by a rota of the Board's most senior drivers who were paid one old penny more per hour over the basic rate.

In accordance with the Local Government Act 1972 the West Monmouthshire Omnibus Board became part of the new Islwyn Borough Council on 1st April 1974. The undertaking, together with all the public works vehicles, plant and equipment became the responsibility of the transport department of the council, its Chief Officer being Mr Glyn Coleman, formerly the General Manager and Chief Financial Officer of the Board. The West Mon bus depot, situated next to St Margaret's Church, Blackwood, remained in use until 4 July 1982, when all transport operations were transferred to a new depot at Penmaen Road, Pontllanfraith. The West Mon was one of the few companies to pioneer concessional fares for old age pensioners, the blind and disabled persons. Any resident who qualified was permitted to travel on the board's buses within the Bedwellty and Mynyddislwyn areas for half fare. The cost of the scheme was borne entirely by the board. When statutory powers were eventually granted, similar schemes were adopted by many other local authorities throughout the the United Kingdom.

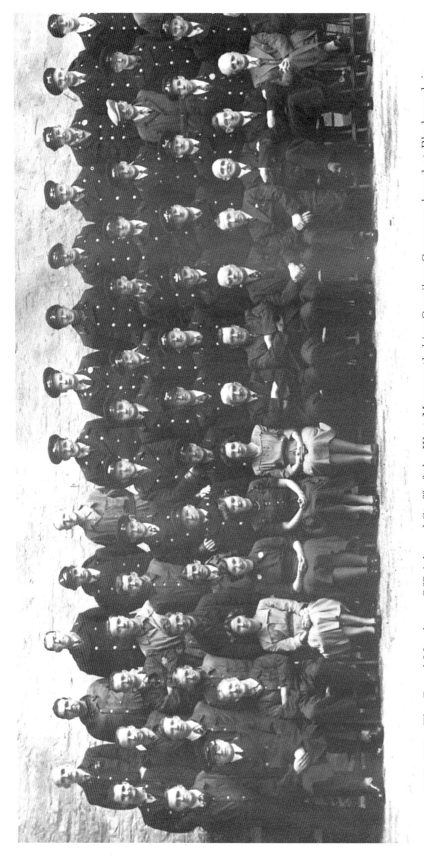

110.-111. The Board Members, Officials and Staff of the West Monmouthshire Omnibus Company, based at Blackwood, in 1951 when they celebrated the 25th anniversary of the foundation of the company. Back row, left to right: W Tippins, D Tucker, K Williams, G Baker, L Evans, G Roper, R Plank, D Bateman, W Smith, L Puzey, W Bram, A Gilbert and J Price. Third row: H Tovey, W John, H Butt, J Smallcombe, C Bartlett, E Powell, E Williams, V Chaytor, R Relleen, W Oakley, I Griffiths, T Haddock, C Williams, and H Jenkins. Second row: C Smith, J Thomas, E Lewis, I Davies, G Tedstone, W Benfield, I Day, C Thomas, G Gibbons, M Watkins, S Jardine, K Tudor, D Edwards and G Gane. Front row: H Short, G Robbins, J Thomas, S Panes, R Jones, J Lane, F Goode, C Pugh, R Brown (Manager), W Alderman (Councillor), E Thomas (Councillor), J Salway (Councillor) and G Adams (Councillor).

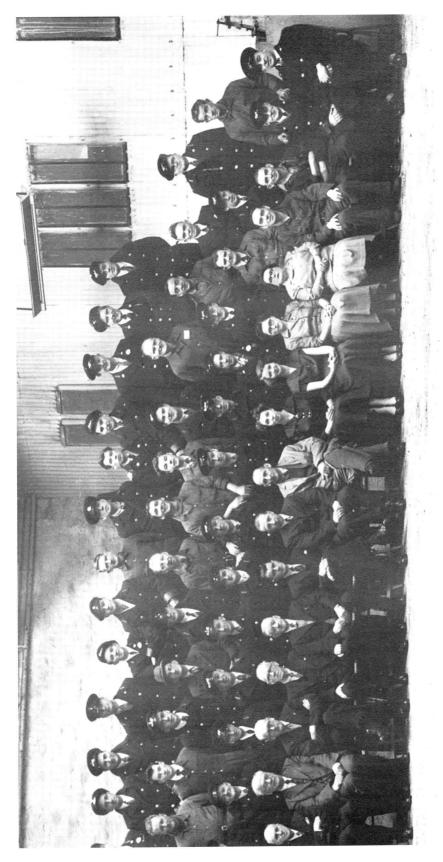

Back row: J Nash, C Garnall, J Steel, E Davies, D George, I Israel, S Lanagan, G Thomas, H Challenger, E Richards and P Parry. Third row: A Salmon, H Powell, H Patience, B Stacey, W Thomas, D Parker, G Adams, L Rolls, D Donovan, R Lewis, W Price, V Thomas and R Cook. Second row: W Lewis, J Mellins, L Jones, B Hancock, V Penaluna, W Noakes, K Gardiner, R Howitt, V Watkins, W O'Neill, D Jones, R Chaffey and S Tillot. Front row: T Griffiths (Solicitor), L Lewis (Councillor), E Butler (Councillor), A Roberts (Councillor), D Williams (Councillor), D Cook (Councillor), G Coleman, B Murrin, O Harris, K White, P Richards, L Walker, E Mitchard, I Thomas, C Walker and E Thomas.

69

112. Hunt Bros. shops at the foot of Pentwyn Road decorated for the Queen's Coronation in 1953. The lower shop, where Ernest Hunt stands in the doorway, sold footwear; the upper shop leather goods and sportwear. Above was the workshop, one of whose products was the school satchel so obligatory for every secondary school pupil of the day. The all-leather satchel cost £2.10s and would last for as long as a pupil was in secondary school. Other important things made in this workshop included the cash bags used by conductors on the West Mon buses.

113. Two beautiful shire horses at Bedwellty show c1950. They are wearing full harnesses which had been made in the workshop of Hunt Bros. referred to above.

114. Two of the Hunt Bros. children, Maureen and Roy, sit on the running board of a new van c1938.

115. A car boot sale in November 1991 on the former site of Budd's New Rock Colliery. The site is bounded by St Margaret's Church on one side and the Drill Hall on the other. The building to the left is the Abingdon Carpets warehouse, formerly Geo W Jones & Sons, Builders' merchants and before that, from the middle 1920s to 1982, the home of the West Monmouthshire Omnibus Company. At present the site is occupied by the Aldi supermarket.

116. An impressive display of Christmas Fayre in the form of meat and poultry at the business of James Morris and Sons, 31 Maindee Road, Cwmfelinfach c1910.

117. The prize-winning window of Woodward & Son c1928. Percy Woodward (the son), C Webb, Trevor Smith, Jack Rogers, John Adams, George Jones, Idloes Bebb. Jack Rogers and Idloes Bebb were later to have their own butchery businesses in the town.

118. A picture taken from Rock Villas which shows the extent of Oakdale Colliery in 1950. This colliery was opened in 1908 by the Oakdale Navigation Company and by 1930 was the principal source of employment in the area. At the height of activity it was employing more than two thousand men and producing over one million tons of coal a year.

119. A view of the pithead baths and main offices at Oakdale Colliery taken by Mr Jack Edwards from the top of No.2 stack whilst it was under construction in 1939.

120. A general view of Wyllie Colliery in its heyday. Wyllie Colliery was owned by the Tredegar (Southern) Collieries Ltd, which was a subsidiary of the Tredegar Iron and Coal Company. The name Wyllie comes from Lt. Colonel Alexander Wyllie, who was born in Liverpool in 1853. Educated at Harrow and Cambridge University he practised as a barrister and became a director of both the Tredegar Company and the Oakdale Navigation Collieries Ltd. Lt. Col. Wyllie, who was Chairman of the RSPCA for the year 1926-27, and President of the Tredegar Horse Show for several years, was particularly concerned with the welfare of colliery horses. He had served with distinction in the Boer War and was awarded the Companion of the Order of the Bath. He died in 1928.

121. Llanover Colliery Argoed was situated on the opposite side of the valley to Abernant Colliery. Owned by the Bargoed Coal Company until it was taken over by the Tredegar Iron & Coal Company in 1932, it was sunk in 1912. During the sinking, two men were ascending the shaft when a valve stuck. As a result the cage shot up to the winding, the banksman panicked and pulled the 'reverse' lever but the cable could not withstand the increased strain on it and snapped sending the two men to their death at the bottom of the shaft. As long as Oakdale Colliery was working the pumps at Llanover needed to remain active. If the water in the 500 ft shaft rose above 430 ft the probablitity was high that Oakdale would flood.

COAL MINES REGULATION ACTS, 1887 & 1896.

Explosives in Coal Mines Order, 1899.

No 7

Abernant Colliery

Brithin, Wni Seam or District.

Richard Jones employed _Overman_ is hereby authorised to have charge of detonators for use at this colliery, such detonators to be issued only to shot firers or other persons specially authorised in writing by the owner, agent or manager in accordance with Section 4 of the Explosives in Coal Mines Order, 1899.

Signed _Jno Ellistn_ March 17th 1900

Owner, Agent, Manager.

I hereby accept the above authority to have charge of detonators in accordance with the Explosives in Coal Mines Order, 1899.

Signed _Richard Jones_

The Explosives in Coal Mines Order stipulates that

(a) Detonators shall be under the control of the owner, agent, or manager of the mine, or some person specially appointed in writing by the owner, agent, or manager for the purpose, and shall be issued only to shot firers or other persons specially authorised by the owner, agent, or manager, in writing.

(b) Shot firers and other authorised persons shall keep all detonators issued to them until about to be used in a securely locked case or box separate from any other explosive.

122. This certificate granted to, and accepted by, Richard Jones, the Overman at Abernant Colliery, Argoed, gave him Authority to have Charge of Detonators. The document, dated 1900, bears some original Abernant grime.

75

123. Mr John Davies inspects a sad sight in 1967. A West Mon double decker bus has careered though the railings at Pontllanfraith bottom station and lies on its side on the disused railway line.

124. The Parrot Hotel at the junction of Gordon Road and the south end of Blackwood High Street. It was a large three-storey multipurpose building which was taken down when the road was widened to give better access to the new bus station. The probable origin of the name is interesting. In the middle of the sixteenth century Sir John Perrot (1530-92) settled in the area, having moved from Haroldston in Pembrokeshire. Subsequently one of his grandsons (Walter) lived in Bedwellty c1680 while another resided in Gelligaer. The family name has been recorded as Perot, Perrot and Parot in various documents. Another Peret (Gregory) became curate of Bedwellty and Mynyddislwyn in 1725 and was appointed rector of Gelligaer in 1729. It seems a strong possibility that the Parrot Hotel was named after this family.

125. This photograph, taken in the 1920s, shows the building of an addition to the main gas works on ground adjoining Glan yr Afon Park. This Gas Works had opened on 9 July 1891 when the VIPs at the opening retired afterwards to the Forresters Arms for 'refreshments'. The gasholder shown here was completed in 1908. Previously a small gas works had operated from what is now the car park behind Tidals Stores.

126. Vehicles wait at the barrier while a passenger train transits the level crossing at Pontllanfraith early in the century. The registration of the open car is AX 872. A delivery boy with his cycle equipped with wicker basket, also waits for the gates to open. The building to the left is the only signal box on the branch line with steps inside. This box had a 45 lever signal frame.

127. The same crossing on the same day as the previous photograph but from the other side. Nothing in the foreground remains today.

128. The 'felling' of both chimney stacks at Oakdale Colliery on 21st March 1984.

129. An engine, with a snow plough in front, standing on the down-platform at Pontllanfraith Top Station c1955. A bus stands on the road outside, behind which is the Roman Catholic Church. To the left of the church are the Mynyddislwyn UDC offices.

130. Looking south at Pontllanfraith Top Station and level crossing on 8 August 1959. The signal box is on the left and the Council Offices are to the right.

131. West Mon bus Number 30 negotiating the railway bridge on Aberbargoed hill, 25 October 1963.

132. The view from Blackwood Railway Station looking south west. Buses stand on what is now Gibbons yard; behind the buses is Tom Brown's foundry and, to the left of the station nameplate, the Carpenters' Arms - a public house almost as old as the town itself. Kelly's Directory for 1895 records that the Carpenters' Arms is 'a commercial and posting hotel with good stabling.' This was a favourite meeting place for 'important discussions' during the first half of the century.

133. Fleur-de-lys station c1950.

134. Advertisements illustrating some of the businesses in the town in 1950.

135. Bus Number 20, belonging to the West Monmouthsire Omnibus Board, stands outside Longstaff's bazaar on Blackwood High Street in the early 1950s. Chappells sweet and tobacco shop is on the right of the bazaar, while The Quality Cleaners, the South Wales Argus office, Templeman's Radio shop, The Dorothy Cafe and the Butchers Arms Hotel lie south of it. Chappells (originally grocers) were in business on this site for the best part of 100 years.

136. A train on the down-line at Markham station in the 1940s. The building is the baths for the men of Markham Colliery. The passenger service on the line from Risca to Nantybwch was withdrawn on 13 June 1960.

137. Elsie Cook stands outside Bernard's Pharmacy on Blackwood High Street c1935. This block was built by a Mr Morgan in 1906 (The name Morgan is set in mosaic under foot in the doorway) and while starting life as a Boot & Shoe shop was used as a pharmacy from the 1930s. This is believed to be possibly the first business enterprise that Sir Julian Hodge was involved in. Mr Hodge was employed at Pontllanfraith station and began this venture in conjunction with Mr Harris the stationmaster at Hengoed. Apart from being a chemists there was a lending library upstairs where books were available for loan at 1d a week. The stock belonged to an out-of-town library service and was changed on a regular basis. This business was taken over in 1937 by two newly qualified pharmacists - R E and A G Thomas. Subsequently the lending library was discontinued and Thomas's took over Booths painting and decorating shop next door and operated it as a book shop. The premises are now used by Lloyds the Chemists.

138. The Sales Engineering Department at the South Wales Switchgear factory, Pontllanfraith, in 1961. Tenders for technical projects for the home and international markets were prepared in this office. Overseeing the financial control of the resulting contracts also occurred here.

139. One of the main assembly areas at South Wales Switchgear in 1961, showing a mass of various types of 33kv switchgear under construction. Some 11kv switchgear is visible in the bay to the right of the photograph.

140. A section of the Contracts Engineering Drawing Office at South Wales Switchgear, Pontllanfraith c1950. In this office contracts were engineered and the work controlled, in some cases as far as installation and operation. In its heyday up to 140 people were employed in this office.

CHAPTER 5

Sport & Recreation

141. Pontllanfraith Grammar School, Junior XV 1935-36. Standing, left to right: Mr Rees, E Lloyd, G Pearson, C Jenkins, E Martin, B James, D Harding, Mr E G Bowen (Headmaster). Seated: K Jones, R Mathias, W Latcham, G Coleman (Capt.) E Hendy, K Turner, M Jones. In front: G Morgan and A Holvey. One of the oldest known photographs of a school rugby team at Pontllanfraith. Prior to 1935 the junior school pupils played soccer.

142. St Augustine's Young Men's Guild, Pontllanfraith, 1924. Back row: H Jones, F Shore, T Tucker, G Hackland, R Bevan, W O Lewis, E Silverthorne, R Silverthorne, S Eustace, M Jones. Third row: A Coleman, J Tithercote, A Jones, S Israel, H Silverthorne, G Jones, A Davies, B Wilks, G Allock, E Giles, W J Moseley. Seated: T Jones, J Bevan, J Harris, F G Jacobs (Sports Sec.) E J Williams (Gen Sec.) F N Silverthorne (Chairman), Rev. B Jones-Evans MA Rural Dean (President), T Sedger (Vice Chairman), R Morris, W T Jones, R Jones, R West. First row: H Turner, J Jeremiah, B E Chicken, H Lewis, H West, W Williams, I Turner, T J Williams, R Silverthorne.

143. The combined Ynysddu and Cwmfelinfach soccer team in the late 1920s.

144. Councillor B E Chicken presenting the prizes at Pontllanfraith Swimming Baths, c1959.

145. Pontllanfraith Grammar School, First XV, 1956-57.

146. The Surface Craftsmans' team in Oakdale Colliery's First Interdepartmental Rugby Match 1948/49. Standing: Alf Morris, Unknown, Ob Owen, Gwyn Davies, Ray Thomas, Ken Jones, Les Lucas (Referee). Seated Unknown, Roy Ackland, Ralph Gwatkin, Unknown, Aubrey Davies, Gordon Jones, Barry Moore. In front: Unknown, Alec Marshall.

147. Mixed Tennis Team, Pontllanfraith Grammar School, 1950. Standing: Portia West, Ellis Williams, Jeanette Morgan, Allan Wilkins, Hazel Cummings, Brian Thomas, Avril Hughes. Seated: Mr Cliff Rowlands (Headmaster), Ivy Jones, Miss Linda Bowditch (Senior Mistress).

148. Pontllanfraith Grammar School Cricket XI in 1950. Included in the team are Alan Wilkins, Alan Rogers and Courtney Treasure. The headmaster, Mr Cliff Rowlands, is to the left of Captain Wally Elliott with Mr Walter Sweet, the master in charge of the team, on the right.

149. The trampolining team at Blackwood Comprehensive School in 1980 with their teacher-instructor Tony James. Standing: Mr Tony James, Russel Hynam, Shane Hall, Gareth Shide, Shaun Cullen, Lee Shanklin. Seated: A Russel, B Shide, Alan Harvey, Keri, Lyndon King.

150. The fifth-year Rugby XV at Blackwood Comprehensive School 1979-80. Standing: Mr Tony James, Jeffrey Cooper, unknown, Stephen Meek, Nigel Organ, A Coundley, Mr Geri Thomas. Seated: Glyn Williams, Unknown, Mark Thomas, Lyndon Hudspeth, David Davies, Rhydian Harries, Unknown. In front: Nicky Williams, unknown.

151. Pontllanfraith Crusaders AFC 1965. The players standing are: G Clarke, G Williams, R Brown, G Moses, B Higginbottom, S Gilchrist, L Hancocks, and those seated: M Williams, I Gilchrist, G Harris, G James, J Edwards.

152. Sirhowy Valley Bowls tourists on their visit to Newton Abbot Bowling Club, 1981. Back row: P Buckley, P Trinder, R Davies, J Lewis, J Main, F Paul, K Davies, I Parfitt, R Partridge, J Francis, D Williams, D Davies, D Brackpool. Front row: S Gregory, G James, K Trinder, W Banes, T Davies, D Gilchrist (Capt.) J Gibbon (Hon. Sec.), B Kenvin, D Jones, T Howells, N Bidgway.

153. Ynysddu Welfare AFC 1984. Standing: M Webb, G Williams, K Paul, D Williams, C Franklin, R Suter, D Collins, S Williams, G Williams. Front row: T Prue (Chairman), S Green, M Dew, I Gilchrist (Capt.), A Smart, J Edwards.

154. Pontllanfraith AFC, South Wales Amateur League winners and winners of the Corinthian Cup, 1970-71. Back row: B Ackland, J Price, J Pask, G Hold, T Filer. Middle row: A Smith, P Chiplin, H Morgan. Seated D D Davies, O Shuck, G Wade, B Leyland.

155. The ladies and gentlemen members of Ynysddu Bowls Club, 1982.

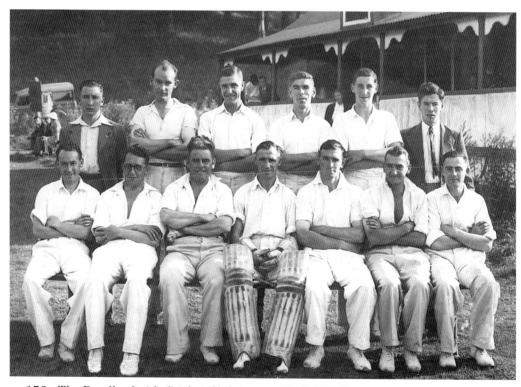

156. The Pontllanfraith Cricket Club team at Builth Wells 1950.

157. Pontllanfraith AFC in the late 1950s. Standing: L Orphan, T George, W Cadogan, D Pugsley, V Crumb, D Williams, G Harris, W Walters. Seated: O M Smith, J Zerachi, J Handy, C Flowers, N Bevan, D Pemberton, V Coggins, J Pritchard.

158. Pontllanfraith Rugby Football Club 1971-72, Captain: Micky Phillips, Chairman: Bill Jenkins (extreme right), President: Milwyn Warwick.

159. Bedwellty Grammar School First XI 1950. Back row: B Price (Scorer), A Chick, J Jenkins, A Williams, W Hacker, L Beard, G Duggan, L Hopkins. Seated: P Francis, M Davies, Mr A Gibson (Headmaster), G Hodges (Capt) Mr H O Jones, A Williams, D Price.

160. Cefn Fforest Cricket Club, First and Second XIs 1975. This photograph was taken at the presentation evening at Porth the year they won the Glamorgan Alliance League. Back row: L Bartlett, D Chard, R James, N Morgan, R Morgan, S Morgan, A Harvey, W Royall, I Davies, K Morgan, M Davies, F Carter. Front row: K Bartlett, S Williams, S Bisp, J Dexter, T Wyatt, T Hughes.

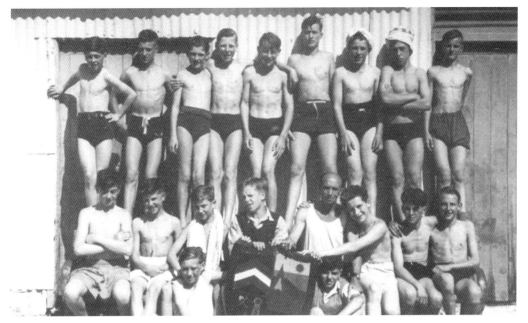

161. St Athan's Boys' Club 1947. It was the custom in the early days after WW Two for miners' sons to spend a week's holiday at St Athan. This group consists mainly of boys from Cefn Fforest. Those not named were from other parts of South Wales. Back row: B Rees, L Bartlett, D Phillips, D Green, G Thomas, D Weeks, T Williams, R Basini, A Royall. Seated: R Williams (2nd), B Lane (3rd), T Morgan (7th), M Davies (8th).

162. Cefn Fforest Cricket Club 1978. Welsh Club Cricket Conference Second Division champions and Six-a-side winners of the Club Cricket Conference and Cardiff area, when they beat Newport in the final. Back row: A Wyatt, K Morgan, L Bartlett, N Hurley, T Birt, R James, T Torkington, A Hughes, R Morgan, K Bartlett, J Oliver. Middle row: J Davies, M Davies, F Royall (President), W Royall (Capt), J Dexter, N Morgan, S Morgan, A Royall. Front row: F Carter, K Morgan, R Hook, C Jenkins Inset: D Williams (Umpire), I Davies, A Ferrier.

CHAPTER 6

Entertainment & Events

163. A car almost buried in snow on Pentwyn Road, Blackwood in a winter of 1982. The 'green' building behind, which was part of the Junior School, was taken down in the mid 1990s. The snow was so severe that the area was isolated for 3 days and soldiers of the Territorial Army were called out to render assistance.

164. Blackwood Comprehensive School Camp 1969. Brian Hardwick, the leader, is seated in the centre.

165. Children dancing around the Maypole at Church Street, Aberbargoed, as they are watched by civil dignitaries. The date is pre 1920.

166. Norman Reynolds as Mr Pond and Nina Prosser as Miss Whitchurch in Blackwood Dramatic Society's successful production of *The Happiest Days of Your Life* in the early 1960s.

Blackwood Little Theatre
SEASON 1958-59

BLACKWOOD DRAMATIC SOCIETY

presents

'THE HIGH WALL'

By Henry Lewis

Wednesday, Thursday, Friday, Saturday

February 18, 19, 20 and 21

1959

OFFICERS OF THE SOCIETY

President: W. Jones, Esq., (Y. Goedlan)

Vice-Presidents:

P. L. Woodward, Esq.   R. Ivor Jones, Esq.

Chairman: Jas. A. Davies, Esq., Redford House

Treasurer: F. B. Watkins, Esq., Hillsboro'

Hon. Gen. Sec.: Mrs C. A. M. Powell,
The Grove, Blackwood

Assist. Sec.: Miss Cassie Jones, St. Aubyns

Ticket Sec.: Miss O. Harler, Laureldene,
Argoed

Programme: Threepence each

Gillard (Printer), Gravel Lane, Blackwood

167. The front of the programme for the first three-act play performed at Blackwood Little Theatre which had been written by a member. Note the price of the programme - one penny in today's currency!

99

168. Ray Davenport, the producer, discussing some of the finer points of *The High Wall* with Henry Lewis, the writer.

CAST
(in order of appearance)

Iris	.	Charlotte Powell
Vicki Hartley	.	Joy Owen
Dr. Tony Halliday	.	Norman Reynolds
Dr. Charles Hartley	.	Henry Lewis
Nora Fletcher	.	Linda Bowditch
Rev. Hugh Prentice	.	Wyndham Scandrett
Dr. Macleod (Mac)	.	Roy Fidler
Alf Coombes	.	Gwyn Beard
Lizzie Hannacott	.	Marjorie James

Play produced by Ray Davenport

———

Time : Early October, 1957

Act 1. The living room of Dr. Hartley. Evening

Act 11. Scene, the same. Two weeks later

Act 111. Scene 1, the same. A few hours later
Scene 2, the same. Five hours later

———

There will be an interval of ten minutes between
each act

Stage Director   George Morris
Stage Manager   Anthony Burrows

Set constructed by George Morris, Anthony Burrows
and David Martin

Back cloth designed and painted by Haydn Howells
Interior set decorated by Glyn Foster, Norman Reynolds

Decor	Clarice Lewis
Properties	Nance Smith
Wardrobe, Margaret Palmer
Music	David Martin

Records and Equipment supplied by Hextalls
of Newbridge

～～～～～～～～

Producer's note :

From the depths of space man tears the secrets
of the universe.

With the passage of time will the secret of man's
purpose also be revealed ?

169. Details of the cast and backstage staff for Blackwood Dramatic Society's production of *The High Wall* at Blackwood Little Theatre in February 1959. Formerly Rehoboth Primitive Methodist Church, Blackwood Dramatic Society bought the church in 1949 and converted it into a theatre.

170. Enid Evans - Mrs Knight

171. Gwyn Beard

Photographs 170 - 173 show four of the cast of Blackwood Dramatic Society's 1950s production of *And So To Bed*. All four gave sterling service to the society for a generation.

172. Archie Morgan - Pepys

173. Glyn Foster - Caesar

174. June Bennett, the Blackwood Carnival Queen accompanied by her attendants in one of the town's annual carnival events during the 1950s.

175. A street party held in Llanover Avenue, Penllwyn, to celebrate the Silver Jubilee of King George V and Queen Mary in 1935. Councillor Dick Vines, headmaster of Pontllanfraith Technical School, is the gentleman in the centre of the picture with a coat over his arm.

176. A very lively group of Blackwood ladies at a local Garden Party in the early 1950s. Mrs G Dyer, Mrs Mabel Dean, Mrs D Beard, Mrs Beard, Mrs F Turner, Mrs A Tedstone, unknown, Mrs Gillingham.

177. Members of Blackwood Women's Institute who took part in a pageant at Grosmont Castle in 1961. Kneeling: Flossie Woodward, Mary Brown, Audrey Phillips, Dilys Meredith. Sitting: Alma Bennett, Alice Bennett, unknown, unknown, Janet Hopkins and Marjorie Kilbourne.

178. Elvet Prosser's Accordion Band who played at the opening of the Maxime cinema c1937.

179. Principals in Blackwood Operatic Society's production of *The Merry Widow* in 1974. Standing: John Cantello, Glyn Bebb, Huw Jones. Seated: Eluned Davies, Jean Pearce (whose dancing card is being eagerly sort by the three gentlemen).

180. Some of the cast in Blackwood Operatic Society's performance of *Chu Chin Chow*, February 1952. The show was produced by Bert Burrows and the musical director was George James. Standing: M J, Ernie Griffiths, H Rees, Garfield Parfitt, Olive Jones, Fred R. In front: Eluned Davies, K Lloyd, D Raw, Cynthia Jones.

181. The cast of *The Gondoliers*, Blackwood Operatic Society's production in April 1971. The producer was Elfed Morgan and the musical director C Butler. The principals in the front row are: Rita Williams, Glyn Bebb, Eluned Davies, Bert Gallozzi, Jennifer Morgan, Trevor Trace, Jean Pearce.

182. Members of the cast of *South Pacific*, Pontllanfraith Comprehensive School's musical in 1993. Laura Jones plays Nellie Forbush, supported by nurses Rachel Bushell, Bethan Williams, Joanne Nichols and Hannah Jenkins. The interested gentlemen are Dean Cheshire, Gethin Thomas, Scott Prosser, Lloyd Harris, Malcolm Chamberlain, Tony Cheung and Stuart Williams.

183. The principals in Pontllanfraith Comprehensive School's production of *The Sound of Music* in 1987. Baroness Schreiber (Bethan Miles), Maria (Mrs Jayne Rookes), Captain Von Trapp (Mr James McClenaghan), Max Detweiler (Mr Robin Hazelhurst), Butler (Simon Wilstead), the Von Trapp children: Emma Rowlands, Claire Price, Lisa Ashman, Richard Shelton, Lorna Robertson, Matthew Evans, Jill Harris.

184. Three members of the cast of Pontllanfraith Comprehensive School's production of *Oliver* in 1992. Oliver (Christopher Maguire), The Artful Dodger (Berian Miles) and Fagin (Mr Robin Hazelhurst).

Pontllanfraith Comprehensive School has provided the community, over the last two decades, with many fine musical productions. This has been due to the drive and enthusiasm of their Musical Director, Mrs Cheryl Robson, and their producer, Mr Gareth Edmunds. Apart from *South Pacific, The Sound of Music* and *Oliver*, the school has staged productions of *The King and I, Carousel* and an arrangement of *The Magic Flute.*

185. This picture shows another three members of the cast of *Oliver*. Bill Sykes (Mr James McClenaghan), Nancy (Mrs Jayne Rookes) and Bet (Keely Mark).

186. Mr (later Sir) Alfred Nicholas, Managing Dircetor of South Wales Switchgear, Pontllanfraith, greeting Mr George Thomas M P (later to become Speaker of the House of Commons) and his mother at a reception given at Cardiff Castle in 1959 to celebrate the wedding of Mr Nicholas's son.

187. Staff of South Wales Switchgear and Aberdare Cables with their spouses and friends at the companies' Annual Dance c1956. This function was held at the City Hall, Cardiff.

188. Wyllie Glee Party in 1938 with their conductor Mr F C Edwards.

189. It was in 1947, two years after hostilities had ceased, that the Government of the day decided that there should be displays to mark the centenary of the Great Exhibition of 1851, in the Arts, Architecture, Science, Technology and Industrial Design; so that this country and the world could reflect on the British contribution to the world in the arts of peace. By 1951 these aims had been realised in the form of a nationwide Festival of Britain, the centrepiece of which was the South Bank Exhibition in London with its Dome of Discovery and Royal Festival Hall. This photograph shows a small part of Wyllie village's contribution to that great event. The 'Vulgar' Boatmen are: Rees Williams, David Edwards, Lon Lloyd, Ernie Hobbs, Ernie Price, Harold Grubb, Wattie James, George Burgoyne.

190. The female workforce at South Wales Switchgear, Pontllanfraith with Mrs Nicholas (the wife of Mr Alfred Nicholas, the Managing Director) on a visit to the Coal Exchange, Cardiff.

191. The Glanhowy Concert Party with their Musical Director, Mr D M Williams. The concert party was well known in the 1920s and 30s to audiences throughout Wales and in parts of England. Never more than twenty in number and all Blackwood residents, their services were in great demand at musical concerts. A programme dated 18th June, 1933, advertised the first visit of the Party to the Town Hall, Cheltenham Spa as 'The Wireless and Talkie Favourites', referring to the many broadcasts of the Party from London and visits to the Film Studios at Elstree. When the film Land of My Fathers was shown at the Capitol Cinema, Blackwood, the Party made a personal appearance. This proved to be a unique and memorable occasion for the town. Back row: George Coggins, J Nethercott, unknown, unknown, H Williams, Ernie Griffiths, Sam Coleman, R Coleman, W Brace. Middle row: Albert Booth, unknown, Billy Garrett, Wyndham Jones, Charlie Vaughan, A Jones. Front row: unknown, G Jones, Mrs D Jeremiah, Sid Morgan, T Hamling. David Williams, the Musical Director, is seated at the piano.

192. The organising committee for a South Wales Switchgear Annual Dance c1963. Standing: Roy Bolton (Production), Wally Staggs (Accounts), George Grey (Accounts), Gerry Evans (Drawing Office), unknown. Seated: Winsor Rees (Personnel Manager), Pat Howles (Public Relations), Barbara Howard (Drawing Office), Spencer Leyshon (Financial Director).

193. An important lunch in the Valley's Club soon after the last war. Note the coal fired stove in the centre of the room and the snooker table in the background.

194. The childrens' Christmas Party at the Woodbine Club, Blackwood in 1958.

195. The hardworking ladies who made the Christmas Party at the Woodbine club in 1958 possible.

196. This was the core of a large bonfire, built, mainly from pit props, in 1935 in the field behind Wyllie Village, to celebrate the Silver Jubilee of King George V and Queen Mary. The man at the top of the pile is, we think, 'Jones The Farm'. Among the girls were Doris Snow, Rachel Roberts, Marjorie Shuck and Madge Liddy. The man with the mop of white hair, in the second row, was Charlie Butler.

197. In 1951, the men of Wyllie Village decided to join in the Festival of Britain celebrations by organising a float called The 'Vulgar' Boatmen (see photo 189). They persuaded Mrs Gwynville Grant, who taught the infants at Wyllie School, to teach them the song properly. The outcome was so impressive that it resulted in the reformation of the Wyllie Glee Party, which had disbanded following the outbreak of war. The photograph of the Gleemen was taken in 1966, outside Wyllie Methodist Church which had been built from contributions of threepence per week by the original inhabitants of the village. Sadly, the beautiful church has been demolished, and in 1970 the Glee Party disbanded, a small core of its members forming the new Mynyddislwyn Male Voice Party in 1972. The Party gained quite a good reputation and attracted many notable guest singers, among whom were Betty Jones and the Welsh baritone Richard Rees. Perhaps the most illustrious guest singer was Margaret Price, who, when a schoolgirl, sang with the Glee Party on many occasions. Her father Glyn, who was head of Pontllanfraith Technical School and later principal of Pontypool Technical College, often accompanied her on the piano. Even then Margaret had a glorious voice, and, interestingly, sang as a contralto. She graduated from Music College as a mezzo-soprano and went on to gain international fame. Singers in the photograph include John Coker, Rowland Paffitt, Idris Parfitt, Enos Bourton, Charlie Hughes, Idris Thomas, Stan Clarke, Jack Cook, Mrs Gwynville Grant, Arthur Rossiter, Mrs Doris Swidenbank, David Jones, Trevor Trace, Jack Perry, John James, Redfus Hill, Howell Briant, Bill Harwood, Frank Shaw, Gus Price and Tom Powell.

198. Locals at Cwm Bridge, Argoed in 1923. Every man and boy, except one, wears a cap. Several boys sport a waistcoat together with either a scarf or a tie. Women attending their washing can be seen in the background. An old inner tube rests in front of the boy in the centre - probably the best 'football' they could afford at the time. This extremely friendly and integrated group so typifies the mining communities of the time.

199. Members of the Embassy Ballroom Dancing Club which was formed soon after the end of World War Two and met above what is now the Sun Valley slot machine shop. The ballroom had a beautiful maple wood floor. Included in this group are A Davies, T Price, D Davies, D Beard, A Tedstone, A Perkins, B Couzens, E Phillips, D Flower, R Flower, S Williams, G Fisher, A Gillingham and I Doughty.

200. Kathleen White, the Blackwood Carnival Queen in 1953, the Coronation year. Her attendants are, Standing: Diane Bell and Cleo Thomas; Seated: Margaret Brooks and Margaret Price. All the dresses were made by Mrs Lanagan.

201. A group from Blackwood who went to Blackpool to see the illuminations in October 1958. The group stayed with Mrs Curtis at 23 Cocker Street, Blackpool North, and include: George Windsor, Mavis Mullins, Jack Mullins, Ray Hoskins, Ron Radford, Bill Williams (Hotel staff), Fred Holder, Les Williams (Hotel staff), Derek Williams, Diane, Arthur Jenkins, Clive Cobley, Mrs Radford, Mrs Williams, Connie, Wendy Williams, Mrs Ellis, Mrs Spillet, John Mullins, Mike Radford, Gerwyn Williams.

202. Mynyddislwyn Male Voice Choir was founded in 1972 by the members of Wyllie Gleemen. In the early years it was often difficult to get the members together because so many of them were employed in the coal and steel industries that demanded shift work. With the demise of these industries, getting members together to practise has got a little easier. Consequently the size of the choir has continued to grow and today there are about 90 members. The choir used to meet for practise in Libanus School but has recently bought Penmaen Chapel and converted it for their own use. All concerts are given in aid of charity, the Annual Concert taking place locally every year in May. A Ladies' Section was formed in 1972 to help in fund raising. Anyone interested in joining can make enquires at the former Penmaen Chapel any Monday or Thursday evening. Back row: John Wintle, Brian Barge, unknown, Tom Mortimer, Terry Davies, Peter Jenkins, Vernon Jones, Godfrey Williams, Arthur Rossiter, Royston Daniels, Brian O'Neil.Third row: Howell Bryant, Ken Gwilt, Michael Coundley, Ernie Marshall, Don Berkley, Horace Hammett, John Williams, Alan Mills, Trevor Trace, Brian Gerrett, Jim Williams, Gordon Jones, Trevor Davies.Second row: Jehoida Jones, Frank Shore, Eric Gwilt, John Thomas, Dilwyn Price, Stan Hughes, Ray Clarke, Islwyn Davies, Reg Tiley, Trevor Price, Danny Morgan, Hayden Noonan, Mervyn, Gwyn Edwards, John Mathews. Front row: Trevor Prankerd, Keith Jones, Arthur Hopkins, Islwyn Lewis, Mr Powell, Philip Gwilt, Meryl Hammett (Soprano), Gordon Gwilt, Gwilym Morris (Conductor), Jack Cook, Pat Bowran (Accompanist), Idris Thomas, Cliff Edwards, Clarrie Grey, Ken Roberts, Wayne Hopkins, Ray Payne, Don Rowe and Idris Parfitt.

203. The cast for the Christmas play at Markham Primary School in 1973. Back row: Christopher Postians, Andrew Rowberry, Catherine Horley, Jackie Lewis, Graham Williams, Mark Vokes, Robin Carpenter, Ann Prosser, Jacqueline Dumbleton, Mark Vaughan, Wynne Hughes, Tariq Awan, Wendy Rogers, Debbie Eyles, Angela Morgan, Mark Powell. Fourth row: Andrew Lewis, Andrew Jones, Judith Powell, Debra Morgan, Caroline Williams, Phillip Morgan, John Dumbleton, Paul Rowlands, Paul Adams, Gerian Williams, Steven Sibthorne, Brendan A'Hearne, Lee Francis, Mandy Fisher. Third row: Andrea Hampton, Sharon Dwyer, unknown, Debra Price, Tracey Roberts, Julie Sibthorpe, Mandy Box. Seated: Lisbeth Grey, Diane Cecil, Sharon Hoskins, Ceri Vaughan, Janet Jones, Lynn Hoskins, Mark Adams. Front row: Martin Lloyd, Julian Vokes, Alison Wall, Donna Vokes, Tracey Powell, Rowena Williams, Diane Fox, Angela Jones, Nigel Jones, unknown, Elizabeth Lewis.

204. The cast in Markham Operatic Society's production of *The Rebel Maid* in 1949.

205. The principals in Blackwood Operatic Society's production of *Maid of the Mountains* in 1962. Peggy Whitcombe, Russell Bennett, Eluned Davies, Garfield Parfitt and Marjorie James.

206. Born in 1970 into a musical family (his mother was Head of Music at Rhymney C.S. his father plays the viola and makes musical instruments, while brother Huw is a Cambridge music graduate) Paul Watkins was a pupil at Markham C. P. S. and at Pontllanfraith C.S. When a member of the National Youth Orchestra of Wales Glyndwr Parfitt, formerly of Markham and a tutor with the orchestra, clearly saw Paul's talent and suggested that he go to a specialist music school. At 13 Paul entered the Yehudi Menuhin school and in 1988 won first prize in the string section of the BBC Young Musician of the Year Competition. At the age of 20, he was appointed principal cellist of the BBC Symphony Orchestra, the youngest player ever to hold such a position in a London Orchestra. He made his debut as a soloist at the Proms in 1993, playing the Elgar Concerto, which was hailed by the Sunday Times as a 'performance of rapt emotional intensity and tonal beauty'. Active as a recitalist and chamber musician, Paul has been a participant at the Marlboro Music Festival in the USA, given a recital at the Metropolitan Museum of Art, New York, and chamber concerts in New York, Washington, Boston and Philadelphia. In 1994 Paul was appointed conductor of the Yehudi Menuhin School Orchestra. He has also conducted the New Amsterdam Sinfonietta. The beautiful cello was made in 1981 by Paul's father John who is now a maker of repute. His violins, violas and cellos have been sold to numerous professional musicians at home and abroad.

207. Mynyddislwyn Council, 20 May 1952. Back: Councillor B E Chicken, Councillor Wiltshire, Mr Arthur James (Clerk MUDC), unknown, Councillor W E Jones. Front: Councillor Frank Withers on extreme left and Mrs Withers on the opposite end.

208. Two army lorries plough north through Blackwood High Street during the winter of 1947. The Red and White bus company offices are on the left and are opposite Tidals Stores.

209. Blackwood Ladies' Social Club trip to Hosegood Industries, Avonmouth on 2 June 1955. Mrs Sadler, a well known local character who lived in one of the cottages next to the Carpenters Arms and opposite the station, is seated second from the left.

Then & Now

210/211. The Plough Corner, Pontllanfraith, looking along Mill Brook Terrace towards Pentwynmawr c1908. The shop belongs to S Morgan, Draper and Outfitter and his window shows a large selection of ladies' hats. A plate high up on the wall advertises that they were agents for one of the country's leading dyers - Pullars of Perth. Below, a photograph from the same spot today.

212. The main building overlooking The Square, Blackwood, as it appeared in the 1970s. Compare this with a similar view in picture Number 7.

213. A view of the same building in the 1980s.

214. The site after clearance following the fire in early August 1991. Smoke damage is visible on the walls to the right. During World War Two public air raid shelters stood here.

215. From the ashes a new, but similar building, has risen. This is the home of Argos in Blackwood.

216/217. The Royal Oak Hotel in the middle of Blackwood High Street, in the 1950s. This hotel, with separate living accommodation beneath, stood on the site for more than 100 years. At the time this photograph was taken, the structure on the right was a fruit and vegetable stall. Later it became part of Woodward's butchery business. Below, the same site today.

218/219. The children's playground near the open-air baths at Pontllanfraith in the late 1960s. The lower photograph shows the same site today. The roundabout, swings and jigger are long since gone and nature has almost completely covered the tarmacadam with grass. Street lamps and telegraph posts have also vanished, as have many of the trees behind the houses.

Acknowledgements

Numerous people have helped in the production of this book, through their willingness to share information and by the provision of many old photographs. While every effort has been made to get at the truth, on occasions it has been difficult to separate fact from fiction. Any errors that occur must be considered wholly mine, and for these I apologise.

My grateful thanks are due to Mr John Watkins and Mrs Joyce Davies for checking the text, to Mr Glyn Coleman for details about the West Monmouthshire Omnibus Board, and to the undermentioned who kindly loaned original material, who helped to identify faces and places, and who provided dates and other interesting information. Mr Gordon Bennett, Mr Norman Chicken, Mr John Coker, Mr Gwilym Cookshaw, Mrs Eluned Davies, Mr John Davies, Mrs Joyce Davies, Mr Colin Donovan, Mr Peter Downing, Mr Jack Edwards, Mrs Marian Evans, Mr Doug Gilchrist, Mr & Mrs Henry Lewis, Mr E J Maguire. The officers of Mynyddislwyn Male Voice Choir, Mrs Cheryl Robson, Mr Gary Rosser, Mr Gerry Thomas, Mr Owen Smith and Mr Malcolm Thomas. Sincere apologies are extended to anyone who may have been inadvertently omitted. In particular I would like to thank Mr Gwilym Davies and Mr Malcolm Thomas of Old Bakehouse Publications, Abertillery. They initiated the book and have a kept a careful eye on things at every stage of its production. I must also thank all the staff at the publishers who have always been most courteous and helpful, and who have made many worthwhile suggestions. The author would very much welcome the loan of any unpublished photographs, memorabilia, etc., from readers who might wish to see the material included in the fourth book in this series. He may be contacted through the publishers at the address given at the front of the book.

Also available by the same author:

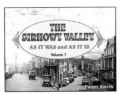